Making Summer Last

Integrating Summer Programming into
Core District Priorities and Operations

Catherine H. Augustine, Lindsey E. Thompson

Commissioned by

The Wallace Foundation

Supporting ideas.
Sharing solutions.
Expanding opportunities.

RAND
CORPORATION

For more information on this publication, visit www.rand.org/t/RR2038

Library of Congress Cataloging-in-Publication Data is available for this publication.

ISBN: 978-0-8330-9924-2

Published by the RAND Corporation, Santa Monica, Calif.
© Copyright 2017 RAND Corporation
RAND® is a registered trademark.

Front cover image: gradyreese/Getty Images
Back cover image: andresr/Getty Images

Image credits—pp. xvi: courtesy of Pittsburgh Public Schools; p. 6: FatCamera/Getty Images;
p. 10: Neustockimages/Getty Images; p. 12: FatCamera/Getty Images; p. 22: RomoloTavani/Getty Images;
p. 28: kali9/Getty Images; p. 32: courtesy of Dallas Independent School District, illustrations by Ex'Zavia
Hicks; p. 38: courtesy of Pittsburgh Public Schools

Support RAND
Make a tax-deductible charitable contribution at
www.rand.org/giving/contribute

www.rand.org

PREFACE

Summer learning programs offered by school districts can provide academic support and enrichment opportunities to students who need them the most. Low-income students in particular lose ground to more-affluent peers over the summer and lack comparable opportunities for enrichment.

To expand summer program opportunities for students in urban districts, The Wallace Foundation launched the National Summer Learning Project (NSLP) in 2011, providing support to the public school districts in Boston; Dallas; Duval County, Florida; Pittsburgh; and Rochester, New York. As part of the overarching project, the RAND Corporation assessed the effectiveness of their voluntary, district-led summer learning programs offered at no cost to low-income, urban elementary students. We found that these programs benefited students in mathematics in the near term, that students with high attendance benefited in reading and social-emotional domains as well, and that the academic benefits for high attenders persisted throughout the school year.

Summer learning programs are not mandated by most states, and superintendents often only offer these programs if they have leftover funding at the end of the school year, or, conversely, eliminate summer programs when faced with funding constraints. As the NSLP nears its end, The Foundation and districts have turned their attention toward sustainability. Summer leaders participating in this project reported efforts to integrate their programs into core district priorities and operations as a strategy for furthering sustainability. We examined how program leaders in Dallas, Pittsburgh, and Rochester conducted this integration work. This report is geared primarily toward school district staff members who are planning for and implementing summer learning programs.

This report is the fourth in a series of nine that will result from the study. The first report, *Getting to Work on Summer Learning: Recommended Practices for Success* (Augustine et al., 2013) offered lessons learned from detailed formative evaluations of the district programs in summer 2011. These evaluations, shared originally with districts in fall 2011, were designed to help summer leaders improve the programs they offered in 2012. RAND completed another set of evaluations of the summer 2012 programs so that the districts could further strengthen their programs by summer 2013, when we launched a randomized controlled trial to assess effects on student performance. The second report, *Ready for Fall? Near-Term Effects of Voluntary Summer Learning Programs on Low-Income Students' Learning Opportunities and Outcomes* (McCombs et al., 2014), looked at how students in this study performed on mathematics, reading, and social-emotional assessments in fall 2013, after one summer of programming. The third report, *Learning from Summer: Effects of Voluntary Summer Learning Programs on Low-Income Urban Youth* (Augustine et al., 2016), examined student outcomes at four different time points: in fall 2013, at the end of the 2013–2014 school year, in fall 2014 after the second summer of programming, and at the end of the 2014–2015 school year.

This research has been conducted by RAND Education, a unit of the RAND Corporation that conducts research on prekindergarten, K–12, and higher education issues, such as preschool quality rating systems, assessment and accountability, teacher and leader effectiveness, school improvement, out-of-school time, educational technology, and higher education cost and completion.

This study was sponsored by The Wallace Foundation, which seeks to support and share effective ideas and practices to foster improvements in learning and enrichment for disadvantaged children and the vitality of the arts for everyone. Its current objectives are to improve the quality of schools, primarily by developing and placing effective principals in high-need schools; improve the quality of and access to after-school programs through coordinated city systems and by strengthening the financial management skills of providers; reimagine and expand learning time during the traditional school day and year, as well as during the summer months; expand access to arts learning; and develop audiences for the arts. For more information and research on these and other related topics, please visit The Foundation's Knowledge Center at www.wallacefoundation.org.

Contents

CHAPTER FIVE

CHAPTER SIX

SUMMARY

Throughout the country, middle- and high-income students consistently score higher than their low-income peers on language arts and mathematics assessments. Low scores are related to lower attainment—fewer low-income students graduate from high school or attend college. Low-income students not only learn less than their wealthier peers over the course of the school year, but also fall behind these peers during the summer. This might be because during the summer, low-income children generally have fewer opportunities for academic, as well as cultural, athletic, and other stimulating activities than their more affluent peers. Summer learning programs can potentially mitigate the gaps between students from low-income and higher-income households.

To expand summer program opportunities for students in urban districts, The Wallace Foundation launched the National Summer Learning Project (NSLP) in 2011, providing support to the public school districts in Boston; Dallas; Duval County, Florida; Pittsburgh; and Rochester, New York for voluntary, district-led summer learning programs offered at no cost to low-income, urban elementary students. The funding is scheduled to end this year (in 2017), and school district leaders participating in this project are unsure if they will be able to attract similar amounts of new funding. As a result, the NSLP school districts began developing other strategies to sustain their programs and the progress they have made in terms of program quality and scale.

To promote sustainability, summer leaders in Dallas, Pittsburgh, and Rochester have made concerted efforts to better integrate their summer learning programs into the core priorities and operations of their larger school districts. We examined these efforts in order to answer the following four research questions:

1. How are summer leaders integrating their summer learning programs into their district's core priorities and operations?

2. Why were they motivated to do this?

3. What benefits and challenges were associated with the strategies they used?

4. What can other districts learn from the experiences of the districts we studied?

Summer learning programs can potentially mitigate the gaps between students from low-income and higher-income households.

Data for this report are drawn from interviews, meeting minutes, and summer program and district documents. Starting in November 2015 through January 2016, we interviewed more than 60 district staff members involved in summer programming in the three districts. The interview protocol was tailored to the interviewee's role and addressed the following topics:

- district priorities, goals, and the alignment of these to summer programming

- summer learning governance, planning, and program management

- various summer programming tasks (e.g., budgeting, recruiting, curriculum development), with a focus on how these tasks were integrated into routine district operations

- buy-in and understanding of summer programming

- competition for and challenges to summer programming

- improvements to and successes in summer programming.

Although we covered all of these topics with each interviewee, our conversations with one to two people in each district were the longest in duration—spanning multiple hours over multiple days. These summer leaders oversaw all of summer programming in their districts and some also led their districts' centralized summer learning programs, serving hundreds of students from multiple schools. Although we also interviewed principals running their own summer learning programs for their students, the interviews we conducted with the centralized summer leaders served as our main sources of information for this study. They were also the leaders of the integration work, serving as advocates for summer learning programming throughout their districts.

We do not intend for this report to represent all aspects of integration within each of these districts. Neither do we think that the experiences of these districts will necessarily correspond to experiences in other districts. Our goal is to independently record and analyze their work as accurately as we can and to identify lessons that other summer leaders might find useful for improving the sustainability of their summer programs. Our findings should be of interest to others who lead or support summer learning programs. We present our findings on why the summer leaders pursued integration here, followed by the strategies they used.

Sustainability Was the Main, but Not the Only, Motivation Behind Integration

Integration involves embedding a program into the routine structures, systems, operations, and practices of an organization. Program sustainability is the primary purpose of integration cited in the literature. A program is considered *integrated* when there is widespread buy-in, expectations of program continuation, routinized implementation, routine allocations of money and time, and a reduction in the dependence on individual actors as the program becomes embedded in the norms and operations of the larger organization.

We interviewed the school district staff who led their summer programs, and they agreed that an important goal of summer program integration was to increase program sustainability. Interviewees also brought to light three additional reasons for integration: to improve quality, to increase efficiencies, and to better connect summer to school-year services for students. As we will demonstrate, integrating summer programming into core district priorities and operations was associated with these desired effects.

Program Leaders Used Three Integration Strategies

Program leaders primarily used three strategies to integrate their programs into their districts' core priorities and operations:

- Build understanding of the summer learning programs and connect program goals to larger district goals.

- Ensure that all relevant departments were represented in the planning process.

- Involve expert staff in and capitalize on district systems to support summer program planning and operations.

Summer Leaders Built Awareness of Their Programs and Connected Their Goals to District Goals

The program leaders who led centralized summer learning programs from the district office strategically built awareness and understanding of their programs among district and school leaders and staff. These actions centered on exposing others to the culture of summer programming. One strategy involved displaying what happens during the summer program by, for example, sharing videos or photo albums or starting district meetings with summer chants or songs. A second strategy was to invite high-level district staff and board members to observe a summer program firsthand during its operation.

Summer leaders also articulated the connection between summer learning goals and specific district goals. To support conversations about the link between summer and school-year academic achievement goals, all three districts enlisted the help of other departments. For example, research departments conducted evaluations of program outcomes. In one district, the communications department used resulting evaluation data as well as data from previous RAND reports to create data-based talking points and a one-page brochure about the impact and importance of the district's summer programs in raising general student achievement.

Program leaders also positioned summer programming as helping the district with specific goals. Two districts used summer learning programs as teacher professional development opportunities, which aligned with a district goal of improving teaching effectiveness. Leaders also stressed the potential for summer programs to help students within the district meet specific academic benchmarks, such as reading by third grade or becoming "algebra ready."

As a result of increasing the understanding of, and aligning summer programming with, the districts' core goals, interviewees noted stronger support from high-level district officials, improved finances, expanded opportunities for district students, and greater buy-in, and therefore willingness to participate in, summer program planning and implementation.

Summer Leaders Ensured That All Relevant Departments Were Represented in the Planning Process

To further integration, all three districts created cross-departmental teams to assist with the logistics of planning for and running their summer programs.

Prior to creating these teams, program leaders experienced difficulty ensuring that tasks were completed on time and that all departments understood their roles and responsibilities related to planning summer programs. The new summer planning structures were intended to alleviate these problems by bringing discipline to the summer planning process, expertise to the table, and recognition that summer programming was complicated and involved multiple offices planning for summer at the same time. The leaders of these teams brought together departments involved in logistical planning for summer, such as transportation, student support services, information technology (IT), food services, curriculum, and human resources (HR), including the leaders of all of the districts' summer programs. In all of the districts, the cross-departmental teams were responsible for logistics, including selecting facilities, organizing transportation, and coordinating food services. Districts varied in both the organization and frequency of their team meetings, but they typically started in the late fall and ran through the school year on a weekly to monthly basis.

Interviewees noted a number of benefits associated with the development of their new planning approaches. One was a year-round focus on summer. The introduction of summer planning calendars, clarified roles and responsibilities, and regularly scheduled meetings ensured that all relevant district departments had their minds on summer throughout the year. Interviewees also described how the new planning approaches improved the quality of summer programming. Joint planning meetings also revealed the opportunity to improve efficiency. In one district, the inclusion of food services and transportation in the planning meetings shed light on how small summer programs housed in large buildings were costly, which led to the consolidation of some programs and savings on operating costs. Program quality was stronger because departments had better information earlier in the school year to support their own planning process. Although some interviewees in one district expressed frustration about the frequency of meetings, all were glad to be informed early about decisions that would affect their planning and believed they had the information needed to complete their required tasks well. The summer programs then ran more smoothly.

Summer Leaders Capitalized on Existing Experts and Structures

Program leaders also recruited district experts and linked district systems to particular summer programming tasks. We considered four tasks that are part of planning and managing summer

The introduction of summer planning calendars, clarified roles and responsibilities, and regularly scheduled meetings ensured that all relevant district departments had their minds on summer throughout the year.

programs: generating revenue and budgeting; recruiting, hiring, and managing summer administrators; recruiting, hiring, and managing summer teachers; and developing summer curriculum. For each of these tasks there is typically a school-year counterpart or system housed in a specialized department. For example, HR departments typically manage hiring decisions, curriculum departments establish curricula, and finance departments write grants and prepare budgets. Nonetheless, in many districts, summer leaders (who may or may not have the relevant HR, curriculum, or finance expertise) execute these tasks with minimal support from others. In the three districts we studied, summer leaders strategically allocated portions of these tasks to others.

When program leaders worked side-by-side with district budget analysts, they reduced costs, thus helping to improve program sustainability. Budget analysts were able to cut costs based on their knowledge of funding streams.

According to the interviewees, integrating hiring into other departments improved the quality of the programs as well. The involvement of the communications department in teacher recruiting in one district resulted in an increase in the number of highly effective teachers (as deemed by the school-year evaluation system) applying for summer programs. Curriculum was also an area where integration appeared to impact quality and also reduce costs. When the curriculum department was involved in writing the curriculum, it was more clearly aligned to school-year systems, goals, and content, which provided multiple benefits. Both teachers and students were then familiar with the curricular approach used in the summer, which may have facilitated learning. By basing curricula on existing materials, districts were able to reduce the costs of buying materials.

Program Leaders Encountered Challenges to Integration

Summer leaders reported challenges around gaining buy-in. Some stakeholders were waiting to make judgments on the importance of summer learning programs until they saw data-based evidence that the programs were improving students' outcomes. For these stakeholders, it was one thing to understand the theoretical link between a district's and a summer program's goals, but quite another to see evidence. Similarly, some of our interviewees recognized the importance of summer programming, but believed

> When program leaders worked side-by-side with district budget analysts, they reduced costs, thus helping to improve program sustainability.

that the districts' programs were not well implemented based on their observations. Others simply failed to see how summer programming aligned with the district's core goal, and instead saw summer programming as competing with other priorities.

According to our interviewees, it was also challenging for district staff to adjust to new expectations and relationships created by the more expansive planning processes. Two districts struggled at different points in this process with determining who had the ultimate authority to make decisions. When disagreements occurred, they could drag on over multiple meetings until it became clear who had the authority to make final decisions. One district abolished its cross-departmental planning team in favor of an approach that involved fewer people in group decisionmaking meetings.

It was not easy to capitalize on district experts and systems. Challenges included ensuring that those executing the tasks had time to do so, understood the essential components of the summer programs, and were incentivized to execute summer tasks well (and on time) without perpetuating the sense that these tasks were add-ons.

In spite of these challenges, interviewees across all of the role groups we interviewed reported high levels of buy-in in each of the three districts, especially in the central district office and among high-level district leadership. Interviewed summer leaders credited their work to build understanding and to connect summer to district goals for this buy-in. It is unlikely that a few dissenters could cause a district to abandon summer programming altogether. At the time of our study, no district was in danger of losing its summer program due to lack of buy-in. However, without ongoing work to maintain buy-in, it is possible that districts might shift resources currently targeted to summer programs to other initiatives.

Recommendations for Summer Leaders

District interviewees believed that integration attempts were, on the whole, beneficial to summer programs in spite of the challenges, and there is evidence that the districts were moving toward more-routinized implementation. Moreover, summer programming was again provided in summer 2016 in these districts with plans to continue the same level of programming in summer 2017.

We recommend that other districts work to emulate some of these strategies by connecting summer learning program goals with district goals, involving multiple departments in early planning efforts, and capitalizing on employees across departments who have expertise in essential areas and on district systems.

► Build Understanding and Connect Summer Programs to District Goals

We recommend that summer leaders help district employees understand the purpose and culture of the summer programs. This could be done by inviting central office and school-based employees to visit summer sites or by bringing the summer programs to life in district meetings through videos, images, or student testimonials. Summer leaders might also ask super-intendents to raise awareness by issuing statements of support, sending emails encouraging summer staff applications, and visiting a program (perhaps with a local reporter in tow) on the national Summer Learning Day.

Summer leaders may also want to emulate the work of the three districts to clearly articulate how summer programs could further important district goals. Collecting outcomes data on summer programs and basing messages on these outcomes might further this effort. By focusing summer programs on key academic priorities (e.g., reducing the achievement gap, promoting reading by third grade, preparing students for algebra), district employees may better recognize summer programming as an important district strategy.

► Establish Cross-Departmental Planning

To ensure that the relevant departments are involved in early planning, summer leaders could work with senior district staff to establish cross-departmental planning teams with representatives from each department relevant to summer programming. These departments might include transportation, facilities, student support services, IT, food services, curriculum, special education, and summer program offices. Successful strategies for organizing these meetings include communicating deadlines and responsible parties for each task through a shared calendar, communicating agendas for meetings in advance, using the agendas to determine who should be at which meetings, and clearly communicating decisions to all relevant parties in a timely manner. We further recommend that one employee have responsibility for managing the logistics of planning and that a high-level district leader publicly communicate the importance of participating. We recommend launching these processes early in the school year and starting with "lessons learned from the past summer" meetings to support continual improvement.

Capitalize on Existing Experts and Systems to Complete Summer Tasks

We also recommend that summer leaders recruit district experts to work on summer programming tasks and capitalize on district systems to complete them. For example, when summer leaders work with finance departments, they can better understand funding streams and how to maximize available resources. Summer offices with strong relationships with district grant writers might increase their chances of garnering additional resources. We also recommend that summer leaders work with communication departments on teacher recruitment, which could lead to gains in the quality and number of applicants. Finally, we recommend that summer leaders connect the school year and summer curricula.

> We recommend that summer leaders connect the school year and summer curricula.

To connect to the right people, the summer office could work with district leaders to expand job descriptions with added summer responsibilities for new staff members. For incumbents, the summer office might consider extra pay, rewards, or workload adjustments to maintain positive relationships between the summer programs and other departments. If tasks can be completed on a flexible time line, the summer office can engage other departments in thinking about when departments have slower periods during the school year and ask for support at those times. In terms of system integration, we recommend aligning summer tasks with systems that work well during the school year, which could include attendance systems, HR platforms, and curricular approaches.

ACKNOWLEDGMENTS

We would like to thank those at The Wallace Foundation for their substantive and financial support. Ann Stone, Elizabeth Ty Wilde, Edward Pauly, and Lucas Held provided valuable guidance on the intellectual components of our work.

We are particularly grateful to the people in Dallas, Pittsburgh, and Rochester who allowed us to interview them and provided program materials.

Several RAND staff members contributed to this report. Stephanie Lonsinger assisted with editing and formatting. During the quality assurance and production process, Jennifer Li, Sarah Pitcock, and Cathy Stasz provided a careful review and valuable feedback.

CHAPTER ONE

Introduction

Throughout the country, middle- and high-income students consistently score higher than their low-income peers on language arts and mathematics assessments (U.S. Department of Education, 2015). Low-income students learn less than their wealthier peers over the course of the school year and fall behind these peers during the summer as well (Augustine et al., 2016). This might be because during the summer, low-income children generally have fewer opportunities for academic, as well as cultural, athletic, and other stimulating activities than their more affluent peers. Past research has found that summer learning programs can benefit students (Jacob and Lefgren, 2004; Borman, Benson, and Overman, 2005; Schacter and Jo, 2005; Chaplin and Capizzano, 2006; Matsudaira, 2008; Borman, Goetz, and Dowling, 2009; McCombs, Kirby, and Mariano, 2009; Augustine et al., 2016), potentially mitigating the gap between low-income students and their higher-income peers.

In 2011, The Wallace Foundation initiated the National Summer Learning Project (NSLP) to expand summer opportunities for low-income students and to understand whether and how district-led, voluntary summer learning programs that include academic instruction and enrichment opportunities can improve outcomes for these students. In spring 2011, The Foundation selected and began funding programs in five urban districts: Boston; Dallas; Duval County, Florida; Pittsburgh; and Rochester, New York. Each of these districts offers multiple summer learning opportunities for their students, ranging from small, school-based summer programs to large programs serving hundreds of district students from multiple schools in centralized sites during the summer.

As the NSLP winds down, the five districts are increasing their efforts to sustain their summer programs and the progress they have made in improving quality and increasing scale. The leaders of these programs recognize that summer programs tend to be threatened during times of budgetary constraints. In a 2012 survey of more than 1,000 school administrators, 35 percent reported that budget cuts would lead to the elimination of summer programs (Ellerson, 2012).

> During the school year leading up to summer 2015, summer leaders in Dallas, Pittsburgh, and Rochester made concerted efforts to integrate their summer learning programs into the core priorities and operations of the larger school district as a strategy to increase sustainability.

During the school year leading up to summer 2015, summer leaders in Dallas, Pittsburgh, and Rochester made concerted efforts to integrate their summer learning programs into the core priorities and operations of the larger school district as a strategy to increase sustainability. This report examines these efforts and their impacts. The recommendations we provide should be useful to leaders of district-led summer programs and others who support sustaining them.

The underlying concept of integration (which is also referred to as "institutionalization" in the literature) is one of embedding a program (in this case, but one could also embed a practice) into the routine structures, systems, operations, and practices of an organization (Noblit et al., 2009). A program is considered *integrated* when there is widespread buy-in for it, routinized implementation, routine allocations of money and time, and expectations of continuation (Eiseman, Fleming, and Roody, 1990; Batton, 2004).

Study Approach

This report addresses the following four research questions:

1. Why were summer leaders motivated to integrate their summer learning programs into their district's core priorities and operations?

2. How were they doing this?

3. What benefits and challenges were associated with the strategies they used?

4. What can other districts learn from the experiences of the districts we studied?

To answer these questions, we examined how summer leaders in three of the five NSLP districts—Dallas, Pittsburgh, and Rochester—integrated their summer programs into their core district priorities and operations during the school year leading up to summer 2015. The results reported here are not attributable to any single district.

Data for this report are drawn from interviews, meeting minutes, and summer program and district documents. Starting in November 2015 through January 2016, we interviewed 62 district staff members involved in summer programming in these three districts. We selected individuals in each district who were responsible for planning for summer programming (either in its entirety, or for a defined task, such as transportation planning) and for implementing summer programming (either in its entirety or by supporting a component of implementation, such as observing instruction). We also interviewed superintendents or the chief academic officer in each district to gauge high-level district support for summer programming. Interviewees included leaders of summer programs, transportation, human resources (HR), student services, special projects, and curriculum offices, and also social workers, principals, principals' supervisors, executive directors, superintendents, and members of district communications, information technology (IT), and budget departments. We refer to high-level district administrators that oversee principals (e.g., school chiefs and assistant superintendents) as *principals' supervisors* throughout this report, and we use *curriculum department* to represent departments overseeing curriculum, instruction, teaching, and learning.

We developed a semistructured interview protocol based on an analysis of public district documents and meeting notes from prior years of the NSLP. Documents included organizational charts, public presentations on summer priorities and results, district strategic action plans, minutes from school board meetings, and descriptions of district summer programs. Study meeting minutes were drawn from biweekly calls between members of the NSLP team and district summer programming staff (we also attended some of those meetings) and also from five years of biannual professional learning communities convened by the Foundation for districts to share their practices around summer programs.

The interview protocol was tailored to the interviewee's role and covered the following topics:

- district priorities, goals, and the alignment of these to summer programming

- summer learning governance, planning, and program management

- various summer programming tasks (e.g., budgeting, recruiting, curriculum development), with a focus on how these tasks were integrated into routine district operations

- buy-in and understanding of summer programming

- competition for and challenges to summer programming

- improvements to and successes in summer programming.

Although we covered all of these topics with each interviewee, our conversations with one to two summer leaders in each district were, by intention, the longest in duration—spanning multiple hours over multiple days. These summer leaders, serving in roles with such titles as "coordinator of out-of-school-time" and "director, summer learning and extended day services," oversaw all summer programming in their districts, including centralized summer learning programs serving hundreds of students from multiple schools. These interviewees served as our main sources of information. These summer leaders (referred to as such throughout this report) were the ones leading the efforts to integrate their summer learning programs into their districts, serving as advocates for summer learning throughout their organizations.

All other interviews were conducted in person and each averaged 60 minutes in duration. We recorded our interviews and took notes during the interviews, relying on the recordings to fill gaps in our note-taking.

We analyzed our interview notes using Dedoose v7.0.25, a web-based application for mixed-methods research. We organized responses by the questions from the interview protocol. For example, in examining how summer programming tasks were integrated into core district operations, we grouped responses according to task: budgeting, hiring staff, providing transportation, etc. We then used the task-specific findings within each district to determine how each task was organized and completed in preparation for summer 2015. Finally, we looked at each task across the districts for a second round of analysis to identify major themes, challenges, and successes with integrating these tasks into core district operations.

This report is based primarily on interviewees' recollections and perceptions. As such, others not interviewed for this report may hold differing opinions. We do not intend for this report to represent all aspects of integration within each of these districts. Nor do we think that the experiences of these districts will necessarily correspond to experiences in other districts. Our goal is to independently record and analyze their work as accurately as we can and to identify lessons that other summer leaders might find useful for improving the sustainability of their summer programs.

Report Organization

We begin Chapter Two by outlining the main reasons to integrate summer programming into core district priorities and operations as identified by summer leaders and our review of the literature. In Chapter Three, we discuss attempts to build understanding of summer programming and connect program goals with district goals and the results of those attempts prior to summer 2015. Chapter Four surveys the various ways districts have established cross-departmental planning structures for summer programs. In Chapter Five, we discuss the strategies for and results of capitalizing on existing experts and systems. In the final chapter, we provide recommendations for summer leaders looking to improve summer program sustainability through integration efforts.

CHAPTER TWO

Reasons to Integrate Summer Programs Into Core District Priorities and Operations

easons cited in the literature for program integration or institutionalization center on program sustainability (Aarons, Hurlburt, and Horwitz, 2011; Aharoni et al., 2014). Integration should lead to stronger buy-in, expectations of program continuation, routinized implementation, routine allocations of money and time, and a reduction in the dependence on individual actors as the program becomes embedded in the norms and operations of the district at large (Eiseman, Fleming, and Roody, 1990; Batton, 2004; Noblit et al., 2009).

Consistent with the literature, interviewees across the three NSLP districts agreed that an important goal of summer program integration was to increase program sustainability. The summer leaders we interviewed also noted three additional reasons to integrate summer programming into their districts' core priorities and operations: to improve quality, to increase efficiencies, and to better connect summer services to school-year services for students. We discuss these four aims here.

Promoting Sustainability

Interviewees repeated the general theme from the literature on the importance of integration to promote program sustainability. Although all three districts have run summer programs since 2011, program leaders continued to worry about future funding and general program sustainability, particularly as financial support from the Wallace Foundation was nearing its end. They also worried about staff turnover:

> We have tried to take everything we knew needed to be done—a lot of it was in everybody's heads—and get it documented. That was one of the key things. So if somebody walks out—say, wins the lottery or is hit by a bus—we didn't want the knowledge to go with them (author interview with subject).

In integrating summer programs to promote sustainability, program leaders worked toward routinized implementation, routine allocations of money and time, expectations of continuation, and widespread buy-in. In Chapter Three, we examine how summer leaders built understanding of their summer programs and connected summer programs to important district goals. These two strategies were the main ways in which they built widespread buy-in.

Improving Quality

The summer leaders we interviewed also described how their integration efforts were designed to improve summer program quality. This was particularly important for two of the districts. One had grown a small, boutique summer program focused just on literacy into a large program offered to thousands of students and focused on literacy, mathematics, and enrichment. Program leaders recognized the need to draw on district expertise to serve these students because the summer team could not meet the varied curricular and other needs of students across multiple grade levels. A second district was transitioning from offering primarily remedial summer programs to those intended to advance learning for a wide variety of students. In so doing, it was seeking to change its image and needed support to market and brand this change.

The most common integration method associated with improved quality was assigning relevant summer programming tasks to district staff with the most expertise in those areas, as discussed more fully in Chapter Five. In other words, these summer programming tasks became part of district job descriptions instead of special requests to specific employees. Summer leaders also asked for more support from other district departments, including HR and communications, to leverage readily available expertise and improve quality:

> [The communications department] did start working with summer for the first time that I'm aware of—I don't believe the communications department and summer programming ever did that before—in summer 2015. There were some great success[es] and lessons learned. The most impactful [result] was the recruitment campaign looking for more quality teachers (author interview with subject).

Creating Efficiencies

Integration was also taken on to increase efficiencies in terms of cost and time. This was particularly important in the district offering more than 40 summer programs. Interviewees reported that the superintendent in this district had committed to expanding access to even more students in summer 2016, and various actors within the district recognized the need to increase efficiencies to afford program expansion. They also recognized that the individual summer program leaders lacked both the authority and the systemwide knowledge to identify and create efficiencies across programs.

When the primary goal was efficiency, integration often happened through merging or combining systems or procedures rather than through creating unique systems for summer programs. For example, summer attendance–taking systems were integrated into school-year attendance–taking systems after stand-alone solutions proved inefficient. This systems integration resulted in efficiencies for data controllers at summer sites and for district evaluators, both of whom had spent time fixing attendance data from stand-alone systems:

> It's a process that teachers are familiar with. [With the old applications for attendance-taking], even though it might clearly say, "Please mark students absent with an X," [teachers] might put X's on everybody that's present. Or they'll ignore the column with student ID, and not put anything in there (author interview with subject).

When the primary goal was efficiency, integration often happened through merging or combining systems or procedures rather than through creating unique systems for summer programs.

Connecting Summer and School-Year Student Programming

The fourth reason given for integrating summer programming was to more intentionally link a district's summer services to school-year student services. One district surmised that students who attended the summer program had the most need for extra support. They tended to be low-performing academically and come from low-income families. Districts have significant resources to support such students during the school year, and interviewees wanted to ensure that such students continued to receive the same level of support during the summer:

> [Our superintendent] talks about summer a lot and the need to provide students with academic and social services throughout the summer (author interview with subject).

Districts have significant resources to support . . . [academically low performing and low-income] students during the school year, and interviewees wanted to ensure that such students continued to receive the same level of support during the summer.

Program leaders also wanted to ensure that students' experiences in summer were continued, where possible, through school-year out-of-school-time programs:

> To make sure students getting services in the summer are intentionally linked to an OST [out-of-school-time] provider in the year. There wasn't as much of an intentional link before. . . . [We want more] support for students who are already vulnerable academically (author interview with subject).

Students are not the only ones to benefit from integrated services; districts might also reap benefits during the school year if systems, expectations, or curricula are aligned. Creating systems for sharing data between the school year and summer could provide timely information for summer and school-year teachers trying to get to know their new students, which could in turn improve instruction year-round. Students who attend quality summer learning programs receive extra instruction aligned with school-year goals, which could alleviate some pressure on school-year teachers who have to help students catch up when they return to school after the summer. In the words of one district employee, "Our school year could be less difficult if we invested in the summer" (author interview with subject).

CHAPTER THREE

Building Awareness and Connecting Summer Programs to District Goals

n each of the three districts we studied, leaders, including board members and the superintendents, valued their summer programs as integral strategies for meeting district goals. In this chapter, we chronicle the actions summer leaders took to achieve that level of buy-in and support for summer programming within their districts, acknowledging that these districts were also part of a national project that included sizable grant funding, which may have helped build support for summer learning programs. The actions we uncovered centered on showing others (particularly, but not only, high-level district staff and board members) the culture and priorities of summer programming and then connecting those explicitly to district goals. We also report the outcomes and challenges associated with these efforts.

Building Awareness of Summer Programming

In one of the districts, state law mandated summer programming for students with low state assessment scores in mathematics and language arts. Therefore, summer leaders in this district believed that they had less work to do to convince district decisionmakers of the importance of their program:

> I think [the value of the summer program is] extremely self-evident to most people—internally in the district, and really to even most of our external supporters, and customers and parents (author interview with subject).

In the two districts without state mandates for summer programs, summer leaders used three approaches to increase awareness and deepen understanding of summer programming among district staff members. One strategy involved exposing district staff to what happens during the summer program. For example, summer leaders invited students to speak about their summer program at central office cabinet meetings, created and widely distributed a photo album of summer learning experiences, and tried to embody the culture of the summer program whenever they addressed other district staff. Such activities aimed to build general awareness about the culture of the summer programs and how they differ from the school year:

> Every time we have a staff meeting [the summer leaders] ask to get on the [agenda]. When they are in front of staff they have these little engagement strategies they do. They use the same things with engaging kids: come dressed in summer apparel, come with prizes and gifts, come in with a chant from summer, bring kids in to get you attached. They have ways of bringing that in and being non-traditional in the way they deliver their messaging. At the board meeting, [summer leaders were] there. They brought three kids with them and talked about summer and [showed] a video clip of summer (author interview with subject).

This approach was also used with school-level staff, such as teachers and principals. In one district, teachers were shown videos of summer program students discussing their love of reading, mathematics, or their summer teachers, with the intention of demonstrating that summer programs can be places where students appreciate and enjoy learning.

A second approach summer leaders used to reach school-based staff was asking teachers and principals to take on such roles as recruiting students for summer programs. Summer leaders hoped that including staff in these roles would expose them to the benefits of the programs and lead to greater understanding and buy-in.

In the two districts without state mandates for summer programs, summer leaders used three approaches to increase awareness and deepen understanding of summer programming among district staff members.

The third approach also aimed to increase district-level awareness by inviting high-level district staff and board members to observe the summer program firsthand. In one district, new board members were invited to see the summer programs in action soon after they were elected.

Connecting Summer Program Goals to District Goals

Summer leaders also took actions to strategically connect summer programs to district goals focused on improving students' academic achievement. Summer leaders argued that summer could be used strategically to improve students' academic performance, particularly for those who were low-income and low-performing: "Summer serves as a way to differentiate our support for certain types of students. Some students need the additional time to master content on an academic task" (author interview with subject).

To support conversations on the link between summer and district academic achievement goals, all three districts enlisted the help of other departments. For example, research departments conducted evaluations of program outcomes. In one district, the communications department used resulting evaluation data and findings from RAND reports to create data-based talking points and a one-page brochure about the impact and importance of the district's summer programs in raising general student achievement.

All of the districts we studied served low-income families, and research has demonstrated that low-income children are more likely to be disadvantaged in the summer, both in terms of academic gains and opportunities for enrichment (Augustine et al., 2016). Summer leaders from two different districts described how they positioned their programs as strategies to help close the achievement gap between low-income students and their higher-income peers—an important goal in both districts. According to one district employee:

> In an urban environment, summer programming is that much more critical because students have more challenges. We need to provide opportunities to catch up, recover credit, continue learning so there's no loss, or experience programming that offers enrichments that my family can provide my children—like going to the zoo or a museum—where some of our students may not have that opportunity (author interview with subject).

Summer leaders also positioned summer programming as helping the district with specific goals. Two districts used summer learning programs as teacher professional-development opportunities, which served an important district goal of improving teaching effectiveness. Summer leaders also stressed the potential for summer programs to help students within the district meet specific academic benchmarks, such as reading by third grade or completing algebra courses:

> One of the things [our superintendent] talks about is reading by third grade and attendance, and both of those lead to summer learning . . . stopping summer learning loss will help with reading by third grade, which is one of his biggest district goals (author interview with subject).

Outcomes Achieved by Building Awareness and Connecting Summer and District Goals

Summer leaders said that building awareness and connecting summer programming to core district goals helped them garner support from high-level officials, which in turn led to increased funding and more opportunities for students.

In all three districts, interviewees believed that superintendents and members of the school board had been persuaded of the value of summer programming. Support from district leadership was particularly important because, in the words of one summer leader, "With so many priorities, [the value of summer programming] gets lost without a strong champion at the highest level of the organization" (author interview with subject). Thus, convincing district leadership of the importance of summer learning is both an outcome in and of itself and a strategy for further buy-in and sustainability. One superintendent discussed support for summer programming as well as the success of the summer office's efforts to align summer and district goals:

> This is a program targeted at some of our neediest students in terms of academic performance. And if we're really serious about our milestones . . . then [summer programming] is a key piece to get us there. We can't get there without addressing the needs of some of our students—winter just wasn't enough. It's hard to argue that. That's why I championed [our summer program] (author interview with subject).

Superintendents and board members also demonstrated that summer learning programs were a district priority through public statements of support. All three superintendents were described as frequently discussing summer programs in the context of district priorities. Similarly, we heard reports of board members advocating for summer programs and requesting information about them in each district. Interviewees described board support as "widespread" and the board members themselves as "advocates" for the programs. One summer program staff member described the increased involvement of school board members in ensuring that families were getting the support they needed over the summer:

> They [the school board] are highly vocal about what we do for summer. We used to give them a report after summer on how it went. Now we have to give them one prior to summer to let them know what we're planning for summer because they want to know and stay involved (author interview with subject).

Along with statements of support, district leadership also demonstrated their commitment to summer through concrete action. Superintendents from two of the districts and board members from the third attended at least a portion of the biannual convening among the five NSLP districts. In one district, the superintendent also sent an email to teachers encouraging them to apply for summer positions, pointing out how summer programs help students grow academically during the months between school years. Summer leaders suggested that this superintendent's emails may have helped build buy-in and understanding for summer programs among the district's teaching staff.

In two districts, the superintendent visited the summer program while in session—one doing so on the first day of programming:

> I think the other thing that I've begun that I didn't think about the first few years is treating the first day of summer school like the first day of school. First day of summer school I'm out at the schools and I treat it like normal. . . . Sometimes all you have to do is show up [to show your support] (author interview with subject).

These public demonstrations of support serve as both evidence of buy-in at the district leadership level and as methods of garnering more support for summer programming from the community. As a result, superintendents were often cited as key champions of summer learning by interviewees.

Along with statements of support, district leadership also demonstrated their commitment to summer through concrete action.

Support from district leadership also affected the sustainability of summer programming, specifically through resource allocation. Superintendents in particular flagged the value of summer programming to their budget offices or chief financial officers, which influenced budgeting decisions. Two superintendents described reminding the district that summer learning was "part of our core program" or explicitly connected to the district's priorities and thus must be reflected in the budget. All of the three districts allocated either general funds or Title I funding to summer programs.

Secure funding allowed for the expansion of summer program access to greater numbers of students. In one district, the superintendent declared that he wanted to serve 25 percent more students in the next summer than had been served in the prior. Another district opened summer enrollment to students who were not at threat of grade retention or at the lowest level of performance on state assessments but could still benefit from academic support and enrichment opportunities. Another district committed to serving students with exceptionalities at equal rates as they do during the school year:

> One of the strong focuses we had in summer learning was making sure our students with disabilities were represented in at least the same proportion as the school year, or 18 percent. Just yesterday afternoon we were reviewing summer results, and last year we had 22 percent of students with disabilities (author interview with subject).

One interviewee thought that more lower-level staff were supporters of summer programming than detractors, which had not been true in prior years. But this only happened because, in his words, "We spent a lot of time winning people over and getting people bought in" (author interview with subject).

Increased buy-in may have led to an increased willingness of district employees at all levels to participate in planning or implementing summer programs. One staff member described such a change in the following way, highlighting how leading a summer program had come to be seen as an opportunity for experimenting with new education approaches:

> I think historically—back in the day—as [a school principal] you shied away or ran away from [running a summer program]. There wasn't a lot of interest. But I think people are realizing how critical summer learning is and thanks to [the superintendent] it is seen as a sandbox and as an opportunity (author interview with subject).

Interviewees reported similar effects on teachers. One program leader reported that 98 percent of her teachers had reapplied to teach in the same program the next summer. Another noted the following, highlighting that new staff to the district are increasingly interested in working in the summer programs:

> Personally it's been rewarding because I've seen a whole shift from my first year when people didn't want to touch [summer learning] or help me . . . . But now instead of that you have some people wanting to be part of it because it got a lot of attention nationally with Wallace and RAND and [National Summer Learning Association], and people are talking about summer learning. There is more research being shared. Even the board is talking a little more about it. It sounds like it's something good, something new, and it's getting traction. There's a fear of not being a part of it (author interview with subject).

Challenges to Building Awareness and Connecting Summer and District Goals

Summer leaders reported challenges with garnering buy-in and support. Some stakeholders were waiting to make judgments on the importance of summer learning/programs until they saw data-based evidence that the programs were improving students' outcomes. For these stakeholders, it was one thing to understand the theoretical link between a district's and a summer program's goals, but quite another to see evidence.

Some district staff did not want to support summer programming without a specific state or district policy requiring it. One district leader articulated this concern in the following way:

> Summer learning is not required or mandated. Many people view it as discretionary. In an institution like this, policy matters. There is not policy that says it must or should offer summer learning, and that's a challenge when the district is compliance-driven instead of priority-driven (author interview with subject).

Others simply failed to see how summer programming aligned with the district's core goals and instead saw summer programming as competing with other district priorities:

> They don't see summer as critical to the core work during the year. Some of the arguments that came up at cabinet meetings when presenting about [summer programming] and why to make

investment were, "How do we pay attention to summer if we have core issues?" (author interview with subject).

Some of our interviewees recognized the importance of summer programming, but believed that the districts' programs were not well implemented based on their observations of programming. One employee described a frustrating gap between the vision and the reality of summer programs:

> There's also a challenge of "rhetoric-reality" gap. Some people want to believe everything is in good shape, and in reality it doesn't look just that way. You see a lot of that all over the district: "Yeah, this is going well," but the reality on the ground feels different. The lack of honest conversations gets in the way of progress. . . . In theory it's enormously important. I think summer is such a valuable time to support students who need remediation and extension. In practice it depends on implementation; it may not be worth the dollars spent in some cases (author interview with subject).

In a different district, a high-level member of the district staff expressed a similar frustration with program quality. She noted improvements she would like to see in summer programs—such as a stronger summer curriculum and higher attendance rates— while still acknowledging the importance of summer programming in general.

Some district staff who agreed in principle that the district should provide summer programs did not actively support or facilitate the programs despite their perceptions of high quality and sound implementation. Summer leaders attributed this lack of engagement to a rigid view of one's role: District staff were responsible for supporting student programming during the ten months of the regular school year and summer staff were designed to support the other two months.

District staff members were also described as overwhelmed by their primary responsibilities. Interviewees made these observations about many district departments, including grant writing and curriculum. An administrator in one district described her curriculum department as "maxed out," and claimed, "they would love to be involved more" but "they are as thin as they can be" (author interview with subject).

Some district staff would go as far as agreeing to conduct some summer-related tasks, but only at the direction of the summer office. One summer leader described this challenge in relation to the communications department:

> I'd like to see [the communications department's] expertise in creating a more robust plan. So I can say, "Can you put this up on Twitter? Can you share this on the website?" and they will, but I'd prefer us to have a longer term and more in-depth plan and for them to use their expertise to guide how we can promote and share our successes and good news (author interview with subject).

Implications

In all three districts, the superintendents had become champions of summer learning programming, furthering prospects for sustainability. Several other district and school-level staff had as well, meaning that more district employees were willing to work on tasks related to summer programming, which we will discuss further in Chapter Five. The summer leaders we interviewed thought that this buy-in was the result of their efforts to explain how their programs helped the district meet its goals, as well as their efforts to convey not only the goals, but the day-to-day experiences and "feel" of the summer programs. Some district and school-level staff remained skeptical of the value of summer programming; we provide recommendations on evaluating summer programs, sharing those results, and using those results to improve programming in Chapter Six. First, we turn to how cross-departmental planning teams were created in the districts and how this furthered integrating summer programming into the districts' core goals and operations.

CHAPTER FOUR

Establishing Cross-Departmental Planning Structures

As district staff gained an understanding of summer programming and how it might further the district's goals, they became more willing to invest time in summer-related tasks, as noted in Chapter Three. Perhaps because staff members were so disposed, they were willing to serve on cross-departmental summer planning teams. Such teams were considered instrumental in ensuring that summer planning tasks were coordinated and completed on time. In this chapter, we describe how cross-departmental planning teams were founded and managed and how they then planned for the summer, as well as the benefits and challenges associated with this work.

Creating Cross-Departmental Planning Teams

Between 2013 and 2015, cross-departmental teams were established to assist with the logistics of planning summer programs. Prior to their existence, many summer planning tasks were completed at the last minute (and poorly) partly because district staff did not understand their roles and responsibilities related to planning summer programs. The new summer planning structures were intended to alleviate these problems by helping to coordinate multiple departments' work.

Interestingly, these cross-departmental planning meetings were not established by the summer leaders, according to interviewees. Two districts were working on initiatives related to project management at the time, and district leaders decided to build their summer planning structures using project management principles and people. For one district, this was an office of project management, and for the other, it was a cross-departmental team of staff with project management training. In the third district, however, the HR department suggested and coordinated the summer planning meetings because the lack of structure was complicating their hiring efforts. HR staff wanted one meeting with all of the leaders of the district's various summer learning programs so that they could plan for summer hiring during one set meeting time. It is unclear why the summer leaders did not take it upon themselves to organize cross-departmental planning meetings. It may have been because they did not have the authority or the time, or it may have been because they were used to the existing structures.

These structures were intended to bring discipline to the summer planning process, expertise to the table, and recognition that the process was complicated and involved multiple offices planning for summer at the same time. The leaders of these cross-departmental teams brought together departments involved in logistical planning for summer, such as transportation, student support services, IT, food services, curriculum, and HR, as well as leaders of all of the district's summer programs (including extended school-year services, credit recovery, etc.). Districts varied in both the organization and frequency of their meetings, but they typically started in the late fall and ran through the school year on a weekly to monthly basis.

Some team leaders invited all stakeholders every time, but others structured their agendas to invite only those necessary to discuss the tasks at hand. In one district, the responsibility to set agendas and notify staff fell to a project manager who facilitated the cross-departmental meetings and ensured that decisions were made at the appropriate times. To accomplish this, he created a summer operations calendar detailing what needed to be done and by whom. Moving forward, all agendas for planning meetings aligned with tasks on the calendar, and the project manager would only invite the departments relevant to the agenda items. The other two districts also set agendas for meetings, but neither linked agenda topics to meeting invitees as rigorously.

> These structures were intended to bring discipline to the summer planning process, expertise to the table, and recognition that the process was complicated and involved multiple offices planning for summer at the same time.

Cross-departmental teams were responsible for planning logistics in all districts. These included selecting facilities, organizing transportation, and coordinating food services. For site selection, for example, facilities departments attended meetings to discuss the availability of air conditioning and the schedules of summer construction. Selecting facilities was seen as a particularly important task to centralize, given the cost implications, as this summer leader in one district explained:

> We did try to do things that were operationally intelligent. . . . We tried to co-locate multiple programs at a single facility to limit transportation and building opening costs. . . . We need to be good stewards of taxpayer dollars and grants (author interview with subject).

Benefits of Cross-Departmental Planning

Interviewees noted a number of benefits associated with the development of their new planning approaches, all of which involved realizing efficiencies. One was a year-round focus on summer. The introduction of summer planning calendars, clarified roles and responsibilities, and regularly scheduled meetings ensured that all relevant departments had their minds on summer throughout the year:

> I think the district is moving in the right direction. Along the way we have made significant progress. For example the area of planning is no longer something you do during the last week [of the school year] (author interview with subject).

This planning relied on districts' capacity to make high-level decisions about summer goals and budgets in a timely manner as well. Knowing that these planning teams could not move forward until some decisions were made spurred senior decisionmakers into action, as described by this quote:

> How many schools? Who should go? Those decisions weren't being made, and no one understood the interdependencies and the impact on the rest of the organization. So this past year was great because we rushed to document everything and made timelines and a calendar. And now we mostly have everything in place (author interview with subject).

Program logistics ran more smoothly because departments had better information earlier in the school year to support their own planning process. Although some interviewees in one district expressed frustration about the frequency of meetings, all were glad to be informed early about decisions that would affect their planning (e.g., the transportation department knew the facility locations in advance) and believed they had the information needed to complete their required tasks well.

Finally, districts found efficiencies in transportation, curriculum, food services, and staffing because cross-departmental meetings covered all programs at once. If programs planned separately and notified departments of decisions individually, these efficiencies would not have been possible.

Challenges of Cross-Departmental Planning

One clear challenge in two districts was the difficulty in adjusting to new expectations and relationships created by the more expansive planning systems. Two districts struggled at different points in this process with determining who had the ultimate authority to make decisions. When disagreements occurred, they had the potential to drag on over multiple meetings if it was not clear who had the right level of authority. As one interviewee noted:

> I think there was some frustration as to roles and responsibilities. The [new planning team members] being involved was a new function this year and it wasn't always clear who was supposed to do what (author interview with subject).

Some also argued that decisions made by cross-departmental teams had some negative effects on program quality. One program leader lost her authority to make some decisions (e.g., about which buildings to use for summer programming) after the new planning structure was put in place. The building ultimately assigned for this program did not have the dance studios and other arts space perceived as important to program quality. In another district, new members of the cross-departmental team advocated for project-based learning in the summer, but the summer leader knew the district had tried that approach in years past without success. This leader argued that if the cross-departmental team's decisions had been final, the quality of the program would have regressed.

Interviewees also highlighted the inconvenience of being asked to attend so many meetings, not all of which were relevant for all meeting participants:

I did not feel that they needed that many planning sessions, and if they did, we didn't need to be involved in all stages of the planning. And because we're so short-handed, for me to take my time to spend an hour or so in a meeting when we didn't have input, was not advantageous to the district. . . . There were times when all of us needed to be there, and that was fine, but when you're talking about topics that don't touch [my department] at all there was really no need for us to be there (author interview with subject).

Because of these types of challenges, one district ultimately disbanded its new cross-departmental planning team. At the end of summer 2015, the summer leader decided to change the planning structure for the upcoming year:

If we have group meetings, they won't be the huge meetings but [will include] the people who do need to interact and have a say in different things. Because transportation's work has nothing to do with food services'. So for transportation to sit through a report from food services and vice versa—I don't think that's necessary. The budget and finance and things that surround that yes, we'll bring them together. But not everybody. I don't want to aggravate people to the point that they are disgusted with us and they don't want to work with us. So we'll use better management of people's time (author interview with subject).

Implications

All of the districts we studied housed multiple summer learning programs; planning for each separately had become problematic. Introducing new cross-departmental planning teams to prepare for all of the summer programs simultaneously was an improvement, but also a challenge. But in the districts that stuck with it, having these structures improved both planning and summer logistics. It led to smoother-running programs, which is important in retaining families and staff who can be turned off by busing or other logistical problems. We next turn to another strategy that has the potential to lead to smoother-running programs—capitalizing on district experts and systems.

Introducing new cross-departmental planning teams to prepare for all of the summer programs simultaneously was an improvement, but also a challenge.

CHAPTER FIVE

Capitalizing on Existing Experts and Systems

I n this chapter, we consider four tasks that are part of planning and managing summer programs: generating revenue and budgeting; recruiting, hiring, and managing summer administrators; recruiting, hiring, and managing summer teachers; and developing summer curriculum. In many districts, employees specific to summer (who may or may not have the relevant expertise) execute these summer programming tasks. In the districts we studied, the summer leaders wanted to shift these responsibilities to, or share them with, district staff with greater expertise. For each of these tasks, there is typically a school-year counterpart or system housed in a specialized department. For example, HR departments typically manage hiring decisions, curriculum departments establish curricula, and finance departments write grant proposals and prepare budgets. All three districts took significant steps to involve the relevant school-year departments and systems in these four summer tasks; in this chapter, we explore their strategies and the results of their endeavors.

Generating Revenue and Budgeting

Generating summer program revenue and preparing budgets are two important early planning tasks that set the stage for many other decisions. In discussions about the integration of these tasks, we sought to understand how involved grants and budget office staff members were in the months leading up to summer 2015.

Generating revenue is a lengthy process that includes applying for federal and state grants, securing commitments from district general and Title I funds, and applying for private grants from foundations.

The degree to which grant writers were integrated into revenue generation for summer varied. Interviewees from one district reported that grant writers assisted with writing grants specific to funding summer programs when asked, but did not contribute to the search effort. In another district, a grant writer actively and routinely worked to garner external funding specifically for summer via donations from local businesses.

The general budget process for summer included identifying the various pots of money that can pay for summer programs; determining the requirements or restrictions on each of those dollars; confirming the total amount of dollars in the district budget allocated to summer programming; managing estimates from other departments and outside contractors for summer work; estimating program enrollment and students' needs; and developing program-specific budgets based on projected attendance and programming, although not necessarily in that order.

In two districts, summer program staff and budget analysts worked together to create program-level budgets for consideration by district leadership. A budget analyst or team worked with someone representing each summer program to estimate line-item budgets based on enrollment and program needs. Once the line-item budgets were completed, they were added to the district budget and ultimately approved or adjusted.

This kind of partnership between the summer and budget offices allowed some programs to more wisely allocate funding from specific streams to prevent unnecessary spending. For example, one summer leader learned that paying for staffing expenses out of Title I funding instead of the general district fund would save costs on fringe benefits and allow the program to hire more teachers or use the resources elsewhere.

The general budget process for summer included identifying the various pots of money that can pay for summer.

Recruiting, Hiring, and Managing Summer Site Leaders

In preparing for the summer programs that were offered at the district level (as opposed to school-based programs led by a principal), district staff members needed to recruit, hire, and train people to run the specific summer sites (typically in school buildings). Each district enlisted its own administrators or teachers to lead summer program sites during the summer instead of hiring external staff. The districts targeted different types of staff to lead their summer sites.

In two districts, staff members outside of the summer office were involved in hiring and managing summer site leaders. Principals' supervisors made the hiring decisions for programs in the schools under their purview—hiring either principals or assistant principals. These supervisors were the same district staff that the principals or assistant principals worked with during the school year. The supervisors' summer roles included structuring training, providing support, and conducting observations. Although we lack objective data on summer site leader quality, in these two districts, interviewees reported that the summer site leaders were of higher quality than they had been before their supervisors were involved in selecting them. And the centralized district summer leaders were freed of this responsibility and therefore able to spend more time on other tasks.

Recruiting, Hiring, and Managing Summer Teachers

All program leaders want strong school-year teachers for their summer sites. Summer leaders in the three districts had some leeway in determining which teachers could be hired for summer programs due to union agreements or general district practices, which may not be the case in other districts. In the three districts we studied, program leaders were able to express preferences for "distinguished" or "effective" teachers based on ratings accorded to teachers during the school year. Summer leaders also focused on hiring teachers who taught the same subjects and related grade levels during the school year.

Various departments and actors played a role in enticing teachers to apply. In all of the districts, a senior administrator sent an email encouraging applications. In one district, the communications

Examples of flight-inspired recruitment materials for summer programming

office created a comprehensive recruitment strategy with a broad theme and targeted email blasts and reminders. The flight-inspired theme included images and messaging consistent across all recruitment materials to create a brand for summer programming. This included "first-class ticket" invitations to strong teachers and references to "boarding" the summer team by signing up to teach. Emails first went to teachers expected to receive distinguished ratings during the 2014–2015 school year, and responding applicants were offered opportunities early. As a result, interviewees reported attracting significantly more high-quality teachers than in past years.

Once applications were submitted, the districts varied in terms of how they involved multiple departments in hiring. In one district, the summer leader made the hiring decisions for one program while HR hired for the others. In the other districts, hiring decisions were made either by the summer site leader or that person's supervisor.

Although each program had structures for observing teachers in the summer, none of the districts chose to use this information as part of those teachers' official school-year evaluations. One district had a structured process for how often summer teachers should be observed by principals (twice) or by principals' supervisors (once).

In another district, curriculum writers, district professional development staff, or coaches observed teachers' instruction depending on the program in which they worked.

Curriculum Development and Alignment

In examining the extent to which curriculum development was integrated into district operations, we designed our interview protocol so that we could answer two questions. First, did the summer curriculum align with the priorities and structures of the school-year curriculum? And second, did the curriculum department have or share responsibility for development of and training on the summer curriculum? In each of the three situations described below, there were curriculum department employees working on summer curricula, which suggests at least some degree of integration.

In one district, the school-year curriculum team was completely responsible for the summer curricula, including the purchase and distribution of materials. Because of this, the district did not have to purchase new books or programs but instead relied on materials readily available to teachers. Curriculum writers provided a scope and sequence for the summer based on areas of weakness identified by district assessments to guide lesson planning, but they did not provide lesson plans for each day of the summer. The curriculum staff also planned and managed the curriculum-specific training for teachers and served as coaches at each summer site throughout the summer months to support curriculum-aligned instruction.

The curriculum department was similarly involved in a second district and used school-year data to set goals for each grade during the summer. As in the first district, the curriculum materials were based on school-year work and systems alleviating the need for large-scale materials purchases. As a result, the summer curricula were largely aligned to the school-year goals and curricula. However, this district provided daily lesson plans. While a team of curriculum writers was engaged in the creation of these materials, the summer office remained heavily involved in decisionmaking and coordination. Curriculum writers attended teacher training for a half-day to provide an introduction to curriculum materials; summer leaders conducted the rest of the teacher training.

The third district took a different approach to curriculum. Principals' supervisors made high-level decisions about curricula for the programs under their purview. Some programs chose to extend the school-year curriculum (e.g., expeditionary learning modules continued through the summer), but others relied on involvement from specific members of the curriculum department to craft new units and lessons. Curriculum writers became involved in summer curriculum writing when asked; the department's involvement was not standard across programs. And because programs had different curricula, it was not always the case that a student's summer curricula aligned directly with his or her school-year experiences. Furthermore, the varying involvement of curriculum writers and alignment with school-year curricula meant that training for teachers was also program-dependent. Some programs continued to rely on curriculum writers to help provide curriculum-specific training to teachers; others did not.

Benefits of Capitalizing on District Experts and Systems

Progress toward sustainability stemmed primarily from involving budget analysts and grant writers in the summer budgeting process. Budget analysts were able to cut costs based on their knowledge of funding streams. Program leads in particular benefited from this kind of guidance because many were not required to work with budgets during the school year.

> It's always been clear that I am not a money person. She knows what to do and how to do it. Some of our funds come from A-funds and also Title I funds. [Grants department] said, "Don't pigeonhole yourself with Title I; use A-funds if possible." So we sat down with [budget analyst] and they moved it around and knew how to do it. I don't know the details; she knows (author interview with subject).

In some districts, grant writers also expanded the funding streams available for summer by ensuring that summer programming was written into grant proposals or Title I plans. This allowed the summer offices to plan and strategize earlier, knowing they had certain levels of funding set aside for summer costs:

> Some of our school-based summer programs are written directly into grants, even into Title I. So that money is guaranteed regardless of the budget process. This has been a priority of the district and the superintendent (author interview with subject).

Interviewees also noted that capitalizing on district experts and systems improved the quality of the summer programs. The involvement of principals' supervisors in recruiting principals to run summer sites was thought to have helped ensure that each site had high-quality leadership. The involvement of the communications department in teacher recruitment in one district resulted in an increase in the number of high-quality teachers (as defined by the school-year teacher evaluation system) applying for summer programs. When the curriculum department was involved in writing the curriculum, it was more clearly aligned to school-year systems, goals, and content, which provided multiple benefits. Both teachers and students were familiar with the school-year curricular approach used in the summer, which may have facilitated learning. And, by basing curricula on existing materials, districts were able to reduce the costs of buying materials (helping to sustain the programs) as well as avoid mishaps with late delivery or lost resources:

> Deciding to use the curriculum materials that they used during the regular school year—that was a big effort to reduce costs and utilize whatever money we had to buy some good supplementary materials (author interview with subject).

Challenges Associated with Capitalizing on District Experts and Systems

The roadblocks we learned of typically centered on district employees' reactions to shifting expectations regarding their work to support summer tasks. There were challenges in ensuring that tasks were completed on time due to the busy nature of district central offices. As tasks were passed off to departments that also were responsible for running the school year, "people [were] trying to think about two things at once—finishing up one thing and trying to do something different" (author interview with subject). The lack of time was exacerbated when departments were understaffed, which was not uncommon in the districts in our study. Some departments asked to take on summer work were experiencing a hiring freeze, which prevented them from employing new staff, and employees described their colleagues as "overloaded" with work. Summer leaders expressed frustration at tasks not being completed on time:

> One of the biggest pain points from last year was [that] the finalization of the curricula was so late in advance of camp—it started

The roadblocks we learned of typically centered on district employees' reactions to shifting expectations regarding their work to support summer tasks.

last week of June, and I can recall that there was still writing happening the week before that. I don't think teachers got their full curricula in some cases until the first day of camp for kids (author interview with subject).

In addition to busy district staff not always meeting summer task deadlines, not all understood the components of summer programming. For example, budget analysts did not necessarily have expertise in academics or school-level needs. One budget analyst reported feeling frustrated because she was asked to make decisions about programming, such as how many support teachers were needed. And although summer leaders were typically happy with the alignment of curriculum materials to the school year, some summer programs actively attempted to create cultures in classrooms and programs that were different than that experienced during the school year. For example, programs focusing on project-based learning or on merging academics with the arts or other enrichment experiences stymied curriculum writers steeped in school-year protocols.

Occasionally, assigning a district expert a summer task meant that a summer leader lost authority over it. In one district, a program leader lost her ability to hire preferentially and on her own schedule, which resulted in some of that program's prior teachers not being rehired.

Finally, districts had difficulty striking the right balance between compensating employees for their work on summer tasks and routinizing summer tasks as part of employees' school-year jobs. Two of the districts enlisted staff experts by paying them extra for their time. However, with fluctuating funding levels, payment for summer tasks may not always be possible. The two districts were experiencing this with the end of the Wallace grants approaching: "I'm concerned as Wallace funds go away about the quality of the curriculum because we won't be able to afford to pay writers" (author interview with subject). As this employee inferred, paying incentives for summer work may not promote long-term commitments or sustainability.

Alternatively, all three districts involved some district employees without additional compensation by including summer tasks in their job descriptions. Some departments found this approach relatively successful, but some particularly busy people, such as school-year principals, felt like they had drawn the "short straw" when they were asked to take on summer program roles. Without incentives, some district staff also simply refused to take on the requested summer tasks.

Implications

It was not always easy to recruit district experts to contribute to summer programming tasks. The work program leaders did to build buy-in, described in Chapter Three, likely facilitated this engagement. But even when district experts agreed to be involved, challenges remained. Nonetheless, summer leaders did not want to reinvent the wheel or work inefficiently when they could draw on expertise and systems from other parts of the district. On the whole, interviewed summer leaders thought that it was important to work to continue to overcome challenges in order to further capitalize on district experts and systems. The resulting improvements in sustainability and quality made this work worthwhile. In the next section, we provide some recommendations on this and the other integration strategies we have described.

CHAPTER SIX

Conclusions and Recommendations

As we have described, there are many reasons—according to both research and our interviewees—to encourage integration of summer programs into core district priorities and operations, most notably to increase sustainability, but also to improve quality, create operational efficiencies, and connect summer to yearlong services for students. In the three districts, integrating summer learning programs into district priorities and operations was a multifaceted process, engaging employees in the central office and in the schools.

Conclusions

Integration efforts were associated with positive impacts on various aspects of summer program planning and execution. Interviewees reported that they resulted in greater awareness of summer program portfolios and increased buy-in from teachers, principals, district department staff, superintendents, and the school board, many of whom in turn became vocal champions for summer programming. Superintendents followed up statements of support with concrete action, setting goals to serve greater numbers of students and making funding commitments. Districts' creation of cross-departmental planning teams resulted in improved efficiencies. These savings helped improve affordability, ultimately promoting sustainability. It is important to note, however, that districts did not perfect their cross-departmental planning in one year. They have made changes and continue to make changes based on lessons learned and shifting department dynamics. In the district where this process had time to mature, interviewees recognized broad benefits. Finally, summer program quality was improved by capitalizing on district experts and systems, although this strategy too was challenging to effect.

Recommendations

The recommendations we present here are intended to help summer leaders implement the integration strategies we have described in this report while minimizing the challenges encountered by the districts in this study.

Build Understanding and Connect Summer Programs to District Goals

- **Bring the summer programs to life.** Program leaders could invite central-office and school-based employees to visit summer sites, or bring the summer programs to life in district meetings through videos, images, or student testimonials.

- **Clearly articulate how summer programs further important district goals.** Collecting outcomes data on summer programs and using these outcomes as the basis for messages would convey how district programs provide academic benefits for students. Collecting implementation data and using them for program improvement might not only further improve summer programs but might convince skeptics that program quality is improving.

- **Be specific in articulating the connection between summer programming and district goals.** Focus summer programs on key academic priorities (e.g., reducing the achievement gap, promoting reading by third grade, preparing students for algebra) to help district employees recognize summer programming as an important strategy.

- **Ask superintendents to serve as vocal champions.** Once superintendents (and others, including board members) recognized the value of summer programming, they could be encouraged to make public statements on their commitment, email staff to encourage applications for summer positions, and visit a program (perhaps with a local reporter in tow) on national Summer Learning Day.

Establish Cross-Departmental Planning

- **Encourage senior district staff to engage multiple depart-ments in establishing cross-departmental planning teams.** These departments might include transportation, facilities, student support services, IT, food services, curriculum, special education, and summer program offices.

- **Use project-management strategies.** Successful strategies for organizing meetings of the cross-departmental planning team might include communicating deadlines and responsible par-ties for each task through a shared calendar, communicating agendas for meetings in advance, using the agendas to deter-mine who should be at which meetings, and clearly communi-cating decisions to all relevant parties in a timely manner.

- **Clarify responsibilities.** We recommend tasking one employee with managing the logistics of planning and one senior district leader with encouraging participation.

- **Start early.** We recommend launching these processes early in the school year and starting with "lessons learned from the past summer" meetings to support continual improvement.

Capitalize on Existing Experts and Systems

- **Strategically reach out to district experts who might con-tribute to summer programming.** Summer leaders could work with finance departments to better understand funding streams and how to maximize available resources. Developing strong relationships with district grant writers might increase the chances of garnering additional resources. Working with communications departments on teacher recruitment might lead to gains in the quality and number of applicants. Finally, connecting the school-year and summer curricula might lead to benefits in terms of quality and cost efficiencies.

- **Turn summer tasks into expectations.** To do this, sum-mer leaders could work with district leaders to expand job descriptions with added summer responsibilities for new staff members.

- **Use incentives until expectations are routinized.** For incum-bents, the summer leaders might consider temporary extra pay (or extra pay that decreases year by year), nonmonetary incentives, or workload adjustments to maintain positive relationships between the summer programs and other departments.

- **Learn about others' work schedules.** If tasks can be completed on a flexible time line, the summer office can engage other departments in thinking about when they have slower periods during the school year and ask for support then.

- **Identify district systems that might benefit summer programs.** Summer programs may benefit from relying on school-year attendance, HR, and online curriculum resources, rather than creating their own.

Forthcoming Reports on Sustainability

The districts we studied were integrating their summer programs into their districts' core priorities and operations primarily as a strategy to sustain them in the face of declining resources. It is likely that other districts face similar fiscal constraints. RAND is developing two additional reports on the topic of sustaining summer learning programs. One focuses on the policy context for summer programming, examining district, city, county, state, and federal policies and practices that either support or constrain summer programming. The intention of this report is to help summer leaders and others who support these programs understand the relevant local and national policy contexts. By understanding the benefits and challenges associated with various policies, summer leaders should be able to both appropriately respond to policy opportunities and work toward policy change. The other forthcoming report examines how multiple agencies and organizations across cities have collaborated to promote access to quality summer learning programs for children and youth in their cities. This collective action to promote summer programming has raised its profile in these cities, strengthening demand for summer programs and increasing enrollment in them.

REFERENCES

Aarons, Gregory A., Michael Hurlburt, and Sarah McCue Horwitz, "Advancing a Conceptual Model of Evidence-Based Practice Implementation in Public Service Sectors," *Administration and Policy in Mental Health and Mental Health Services Research*, Vol. 38, No. 1, January 2011, pp. 4–23.

Aharoni, Eyal, Lila Rabinovich, Joshua Mallett, and Andrew R. Morral, *An Assessment of Program Sustainability in Three Bureau of Justice Assistance Criminal Justice Domains*, Santa Monica, Calif.: RAND Corporation, RR-550-BJA, 2014. As of May 4, 2017:
https://www.rand.org/pubs/research_reports/RR550.html

Augustine, Catherine H., Jennifer Sloan McCombs, John F. Pane, Heather L. Schwartz, Jonathan Schweig, Andrew McEachin, and Kyle Siler-Evans, *Learning from Summer: Effects of Voluntary Summer Learning Programs on Low-Income Urban Youth*, Santa Monica, Calif.: RAND Corporation, RR-1557-WF, 2016. As of December 5, 2016:
http://www.rand.org/pubs/research_reports/RR1557.html

Augustine, Catherine H., Jennifer Sloan McCombs, Heather L. Schwartz, and Laura Zakaras, *Getting to Work on Summer Learning: Recommended Practices for Success*, Santa Monica, Calif.: RAND Corporation, RR-366-WF, 2013. As of March 18, 2016:
http://www.rand.org/pubs/research_reports/RR366.html

Batton, Jennifer, "Commentary: Considering Conflict Resolution Education: Next Steps for Institutionalization," *Conflict Resolution Quarterly*, Vol. 22, Nos. 1–2, 2004, pp. 269–278.

Borman, Geoffrey D., James Benson, and Laura T. Overman, "Families, Schools, and Summer Learning," *Elementary School Journal*, Vol. 106, November 2005, pp. 131–150.

Borman, Geoffrey D., Michael Goetz, and N. Maritza Dowling, "Halting the Summer Achievement Slide: A Randomized Field Trial of the KindergARTen Summer Camp," *Journal of Education for Students Placed at Risk (JESPAR)*, Vol. 14, No. 2, April 2009, pp. 133–147.

Chaplin, Duncan, and Jeffrey Capizzano, *Impacts of a Summer Learning Program: A Random Assignment Study of Building Educated Leaders for Life (BELL)*, Washington, D.C.: Urban Institute, 2006.

Eiseman, Jeffrey W., Douglas S. Fleming, and Deborah S. Roody, "Making Sure It Sticks: The School Improvement Leader's Role in Institutionalizing Change," in Jeffrey W. Eiseman, ed., *The School Improvement Leader: Four Perspectives on Change in Schools*, Andover, Mass.: Regional Laboratory for Educational Improvement, 1990.

Ellerson, Noelle M., *Cut Deep: How the Sequester Will Impact Our Nation's Schools*, Alexandria, Va.: American Association of School Administrators, July 2012.

Jacob, Brian A., and Lars Lefgren, "Remedial Education and Student Achievement: A Regression-Discontinuity Design," *Review of Economics and Statistics*, Vol. 86, No. 1, February 2004, pp. 226–244.

Matsudaira, Jordan D., "Mandatory Summer School and Student Achievement," *Journal of Econometrics*, Vol. 142, No. 2, February 2008, pp. 829–850.

McCombs, Jennifer Sloan, Sheila Nataraj Kirby, and Louis T. Mariano, eds., *Ending Social Promotion Without Leaving Children Behind: The Case of New York City*, Santa Monica, Calif.: RAND Corporation, MG-894-NYCDOE, 2009. As of March 21, 2016:
http://www.rand.org/pubs/monographs/MG894.html

McCombs, Jennifer Sloan, John F. Pane, Catherine H. Augustine, Heather L. Schwartz, Paco Martorell, and Laura Zakaras, *Ready for Fall? Near-Term Effects of Voluntary Summer Learning Programs on Low-Income Students' Learning Opportunities and Outcomes*, Santa Monica, Calif.: RAND Corporation, RR-815-WF, 2014. As of March 18, 2016:
http://www.rand.org/pubs/research_reports/RR815.html

Noblit, George W., H. Dickson Corbett, Bruce L. Wilson, and Monica B. McKinney, *Creating and Sustaining Arts-Based School Reform: The A+ Schools Program*, Abingdon, England: Taylor & Francis, 2009.

Schacter, John, and Booil Jo, "Learning When School Is Not in Session: A Reading Summer Day-Camp Intervention to Improve the Achievement of Exiting First-Grade Students Who Are Economically Disadvantaged," *Journal of Research in Reading*, Vol. 28, No. 2, 2005, pp. 158–169.

U.S. Department of Education, "2015 Mathematics and Reading Assessments," nationsreportcard.gov, 2015. As of April 12, 2016: http://www.nationsreportcard.gov/reading_math_2015/#?grade=4